wildflowers

Wildflowers

Poems by
Sierra Lewis

ISBN-10 1-6379-0396-0
ISBN-13 978-1-6379-0396-4

Published May 2022

a collection of emotions
meant to stir a commotion,
inside of your heart

a delicate hand, holds a pen
struggling to decide, where to begin
a delicate soul... looks to the wind
the soft touch caresses her skin
a deep breathe - a pause - a hold
in this moment, she knows - it is finally time,
to let her story be told
to finally... let go

when you read the words
your hands have written

the tears stream
from your eyes
it comes as a
surprise

the decision to let it out,
all that has been hidden for all of time

i fear to be seen,
without really ever being seen
i fear to be listened to
without ever being heard
i fear to make sense and
never be understood
i would take your hand and show you if i could
i fear to be completely myself,
to get lost in a sea of everyone else
i like to be alone, just on my own
the lines start to blur,
my heart starts to stir
what would i do?
if all of this came true?

i go through everyday
pretending that i am okay,
but i'm not... or i wasn't

i stand here with a smile
on my face, a laugh for all
of their jokes
but they would never know

at night, when i'm home alone
i choke on my tears,
tears i've been holding in
for so many years
a sadness i can't let go
because if i let it go,
i'll have nothing left to hold
that reminds me of you
that feeling i learned to keep close
when i was only five years old

a feeling, an emotion...
words that could never be spoken
until now, because i am beyond broken
my heart is so heavy, i can't hold it anymore

you can't even out this score
i'm here and you're gone
year after year goes by
and i realize,
that will never change,
even if we could turn back time,
it wouldn't make a difference,
because i am here, exactly...
where i need to be...

pouring out these words for the world to see
and there you are up above, watching down over me.
the loss of you has shaped and molded everything i was,
everything i have become, so misunderstood for so long
i misunderstood myself and the feelings i had,
my body was protecting myself from the pain to be had

awareness began to set in, piece by piece
mend by mend
here i am with tears on my cheeks
i finally know how to begin,
how to begin truly living
week by week i see what a blessing life has given me
no burden to big, no task to hard

i just look to the sky,
and... there you are

i am here, i miss you more than any word...
could ever define, but i hope you are proud
that i am yours and you will always be mine.

it's in these moments...
i realize what i fear the most,
what's really left?
pieces of me?
or am i just a ghost
a ghost of who i used to be
just grasping for a thread of reality,
who really knows?

i think in poems,
i speak in silence
i've mastered the art,
as if it were a science
here we are-stuck in the chaos,
would anyone know?
it's always so quiet...

i never speak of you,
not by name
i refuse to admit, the mess
you left behind
the parts of me,
that no longer remain

sometimes, i think of you
the universe in your eyes
that i cling to
blue, orange and gold
speckled throughout
the memories i hold
eye to eye - soul to soul
our lips meet - and i let go
let go - of fear - of love - of lust
i lose it all in the thought of us
i see you and worlds collide
all the colors in your eyes
no sense of earth - or space - or time
all found... and then lost

finally grasping that you,
will never be mine

thoughts and perceptions,
perceptions and thoughts
they are what they are
they are what they're not
a million point of views,
a million views of you
                it's all the same,
except that it's not
contradictions and confirmations
who's to say which is which
                and which is not
thoughts and perceptions,
perceptions and thoughts

a simple delicate sound
falls so softly,
off your lips

i watch as they move
so slowly,
down my hips

i inhale,
as i feel
the words unspoken

how do you
make me feel,
so unbroken?

like soft whispers
against my skin
reassuring me
again and again

something about the
intimacy of symmetry
the architecture of foreign buildings
and your face,
jawlines and high ceilings
with beams in place
perfectly symmetrical,
everything in its right place
...all of the lines that i love to trace

a moment in time...
when your eyes... held mine
longer than most have lived
a thousand lives i lived in your eyes
a moment, an eternity...
what is it that you do to me...
i'd die a thousand more times
to live in the moment
your eyes met mine

i'll be forever searching for a way,
to immortalize...
all of the colors in your eyes

he came and left
as quickly as the wind
on a warm summer day

she was forever lost in the complexity
with which he stays

i made up my own
truths about you
so believable,
you even thought them true
now i get to mourn the you,
the you i always wish i knew

a love that hurts
really isn't love at all is it?
just a portion or a notion...
after all, infatuation
seems to be all the commotion

i just want to crawl inside
and turn the light on inside of your mind
I feel at home surrounded by your thoughts
now here is a place, that I'd love to be lost

i swallow you down,
every last lie you speak,
blue eyes and beautiful whispers
you make me feel so weak...
i can feel you course through my veins
so slowly we coalesce,
until i'm yours to keep.

always hiding behind facades
only showing the happy parts
being suppressed for decades
just waiting to be ripped apart
you should receive all of the accolades
you're the master of the art
never to be really seen,
hiding everything from the start

"we will always have paris..." he whispered.
in that moment
the weight of a thousand worlds
came crashing down
... on her heart
destruction of all its finest parts
the string of quantum entanglement
had been severed
just as quickly as it was wound
the fabric of her being
unraveling as she fell to the ground

how many times,
can the same person rip you apart?
how many times did that same person,
captivate your heart?
how many times more until you realize
they aren't who they were at the start

shedding skin, shedding tears
even after all of these years
transformation after transformation
shedding skins
shedding tears,
but i still can't shed you after all of these years

"i don't think i want you in my life anymore..."
it came out as a gasp,
a gasp for more air
a gasp for life without you there
a thought - a moment
just one minute without you in it
i've always wondered what a life like that would be?
it... is a necessity,
not a dream
what could this possibly mean?
i can't remain caught here in your gaze for eternity,
in this moment in time
i beg you to set me free
it's not me, it's you - that fails to see
what it is that you seek
let me go and i'll show you what it is you need

i miss the you,
the you that you are

you can't hide from me,
i saw you from the start...

i search for you
in the city streets
the lights of the skyline,
lost on me
all of the faces a blur
searching for...
a pair of cheekbones
a universe in their eyes,
none of them quite matching
your portrait of lies

an ember is only born in the death of a fire
it glows just enough to resemble desire
last remaining light, right before the dark
the last remaining light inside of my tired heart

this enigmatic feeling, pulsing through my veins
everything feels so lucid, how can this be explained
the wildest of fires will always be put out, but
before that, an ember flickers
as the last of hope runs out

they glow and fall to ash,
smolder and flash
last remaining light, right before the dark
the last remaining warmth inside of my tired heart
this enigmatic feeling pulsing through my veins

everything felt so real, how can this be explained
the wildest of fires will always have an end
but before that - an ember - a glow before the mend

all things left untold
to heavy to hold
i just want to let them go..
before i lose control
spiraling into dimensions unknown,
dimensions unseen
will you catch me?
a keeper of thoughts is what i need
a real release
all these thoughts and memories
to heavy to hold
until i finally let them go
time to let you go...

i heard some news today,
news i thought i couldn't take
to my surprise,
there was no ache
no ache, for you
or that place
i'm happy to see a smiling face
you were never meant to be more,
than a holding space

she withers and wilts,
falls to the ground...
petals so light, they don't make a sound
between his fingers, she crumbles
lost in the wind...

far away the essence of her blows,
only to be born again

the warmth of the water
flushing my pale skin
you behind me,
taking me in
hearts racing -then calm
here we were,
palm to palm
i could feel your breath
against my skin
enticing my need
to breathe you in
soul to soul -eye to eye
here we moved -
so intricately entwined

all i could do was follow you home
to the mountains, to the cold
as your sun rises, so does mine set
as you wake, i lay my head to rest
all i want is to follow you home
home to the mountains, home to the cold
home to your lips, home to your kiss
home to my heart and yours,
which i dearly miss.

i dream of night walks
through brightly lit cities

freezing cold air,
dissipated by the warmest touch

i dream of you,
i dream of us

sometimes, the things
you need most
aren't things at all,
or people
sometimes all you need
is a perfect sunset
on a mountainside
in a foreign land

i rediscover you a little each day,
i hear your words and change your ways,
i resist your urge to stay the same
i see your truth as it makes its way
a grand debut, you could say
because i am you...
one in the same

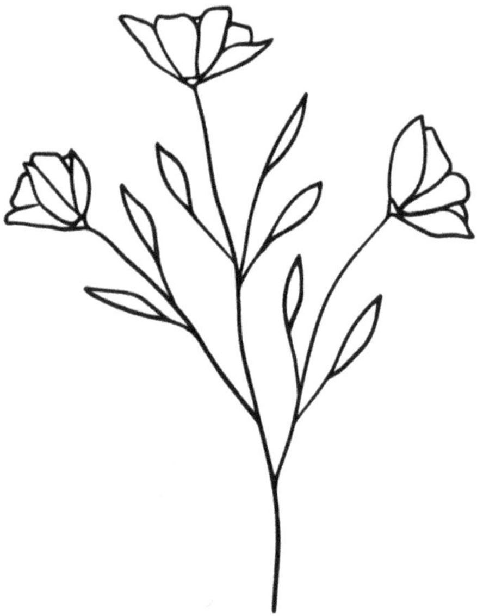

every morning i wake
and look to see
to see you, in the mirror
staring back at me
i see your smile, so wide
the gold reflecting in your eyes
a fiery soul survived
it dwells so deeply inside
inside of you?
or is it me?
to akin to see, give me clarity?
there you are
and here i am
so far apart, but here we stand
there can be no me without you
a fiery soul that i could never lose

intricacies of genuity
so beautiful i could trace
trace the skin,
so gently on your face
don't say a thing,
don't move a blink
just take a breath, a break
don't even think

we are never alone,
just as the wolves howl...
we all dream to the same moon
look to the sky,
see how she shines for you

lost in your touch -surroundings a blur
warmed by your tan skin and the feeling of fur

here i lay upon my bed,
a million thoughts whirling inside my head
feeling so tired and weak,
as these tears roll down my cheeks
eyes, eyes tired from the exhaustion of the week
feeling so delicate and human
humbling, to say the least

loss is inevitable,
like the leaves on trees
the seasons come and go
and time barrels on
living in the moments
while they're here and
appreciating them
when they're gone

so many hurdles have been made,
in these past years i have paved the way
gains and losses day after day
only to find that i have less to say
less to say and more to know
isn’t that how the lessons go?
one day we live and one day we learn
it's this life that i thrive to earn
up and down mountains, through valleys and snow,
here’s where i found what i needed to know
lost in a field with a sky full of stars... here lies the answer...
so close but so far
it's not where we once were but here,
where we are

it is a magical thing, letting go.
it is only here in this space
that we truly know...
know the feeling
the free fall,
that inevitable feeling,
that began it all.

rejuvenate my soul
with the silence of the trees
the serenity of the fresh mountain breeze
the smell of new rain as it dances from the sky above
my thought filled mind quieted with love
to be washed clean
all worries vanish, as each drop reaches my skin
gratitude grows as the trees take me in

i sit here and stare out the window at the trees,
its as if they are staring right back at me

sometimes, they make me feel
like i'm in a distant place and
none of this is real
it fills me with a magic i just can't place

old memories fill my mind,
memories of a simpler time
it is here and now,
that i am so grateful for the happiness
that those memories provide
a time when we were free to walk outside

the thunder roaring in the distance
the rhythmic sound of raindrops - falling
fills my ears
here is where i find solace -
alone with my thoughts, after all of these years
taking walks through the maze in my mind,
enveloped by emotion, no sense of time
i prefer the silence, where only nature speaks
a beautiful composure, a tranquility to blend with mine
a place that the soul always seeks
but is so hard to find

walking through the forest
surrounded by the crisp air
i can feel the breeze lightly rustle my hair
the melodic sound of birds singing,
squirrels darting around without a care
you can spend your whole life looking
only to realize that you're already there

palm trees swaying in the wind
raindrops pat pattering on the leaves
again and again
a sort of calm before the storm
your thoughts are beginning to look so worn

"rest now" she whispers
"this is all soon to end,

...before we know it , we will all begin to mend"

all of the primary colors
red, yellow, green and blue
no mix of them could ever
capture the essence of you

to have and to hold,
and always let go

i get this nagging feeling,
it sneaks up from time to time
i get this nagging feeling
because i've always felt
that you'd be mine
i get this nagging feeling
because here i sit, alone
i get this nagging feeling
and i know
it's not my own

grow and be bold
do not fear growing old
be true and let it show
they will never know if they're never told
wisdom in tears, wisdom in years
a story kept isn't a story told
a flower blooms as the seed grows
say it out loud, and let it all go.

my mind is always trying
to translate the complexities
of my heart

only for the mediocre minds
to pick them apart

the art of surrender
such a liberating notion,
a vibrant vulnerability
an invitation
a synchronistic flow of movements
set into motion
a boundless vindication

i can see it in your eyes
the inexhaustible vulnerability
you don't try to hide

you hold the power,
the power to thrive

honesty at your core,
a radiance that i cannot ignore

so hard to resist,
let your light shine,
it's so nice to know that you exist

slow down enough
to enjoy the array of colors
of a sunset in late fall

slow down enough
to enjoy the still moments

slow down enough
to feel it all

she smells of lilacs and lilies
soft to the touch and oh so pretty
she turns towards her sun,
she finds him so peculiar, really
warmed by his light
she could watch him for hours,
even into the night...
oh, wildflower

show me all of the things you hold deep inside,
show me all of the things you try to hide...
if you show me yours,
i'll show you mine
what life is to live,
if you can never let someone inside

let there be dark
just follow the light
i will always follow you into the night
feel the depths of my soul -
hold me so tight
i don't want to breathe,
until we feel the warmth of morning light

i could inscribe your name on the bottom
of every page,
so that you knew... they were meant for you
with every word i'm in debt to you
if you only knew the way that i felt for you
with knowledge comes awareness
but there is beauty in the secrets
so i bask here in the stillness
i'll never leave the quiet
i've fallen in love with the silence

when i move, you move
things are so fluid with you
as if we were one, not two
you make me lighter
you take me higher, then i've ever been
all in, with nothing to lose
come here and set this fire...
i have nothing left to lose
except for you

i could write an entire language of my own,
so i could better describe
the feelings that live inside
so foreign from anything or anyone...
that has stepped foot on this plane
but yet, you feel like home
a reality still waiting to be explained

my face tucked in your neck
our legs intertwined -
the perfect body,
to meld with mine

i could lay here for hours
and pass the time
the sound of your heart,
beat for beat
perfectly in sync with mine

lulled to rest
wrapped around you
what a lovely place to be
here, in this moment of time

i love to listen
to all of the noises you don't know that you make
i love to give to you - and not take
trying to provide enough space,
for you to be you
without too much ache
hold me close -
for your own sake
i want to let go,
but it's too late

trying to learn how to feel
trying to tell if this is even real?
what are these emotions that i hold?
will they forever be left untold?
will you see me for who i really am?
even if i can't see myself?
is this all part of your master plan?
should i put this to the test?
is this a cry for help?
is this really for the best?

i left traces of my fingerprints
all over your skin,
ingrained in your mind
my identity left behind -
in your thoughts
and you wonder why i
i'm feeling so lost...

who am i, without you?

small moments of joy, eternal bliss
these tangible moments, with you
will be so dearly missed
a breathtaking journey, so true
lips that should often be kissed - by you
an ethereal instant,
too quickly dismissed

i reach to my neck,
just to check
is it still beating?
so slowly it pulses
i can feel the heat - as it rises
into my chest - up to my eyes
the tears form,
they fall from the skies
the rise and fall of breath -
irrefutable proof
of life and not death

she holds the sadness
of a thousand years
inside of her heart

never sheds a tear,
a warrior from the start

a beautiful timeless face...
a portrait of art
each stroke of paint
burying all of her scars

slight shifts in perception
a leisurely afternoon walk
a subtle drift in connection
a lovely intimate talk
monumental shifts in direction
it's not often that simplicity steers perfection.

welcome to the secret garden of mystery and wonder
beware of its spell, it will pull you under
there is no air to breathe,
choked by passion
and then she leaves...
disappears, amongst the flowers and trees

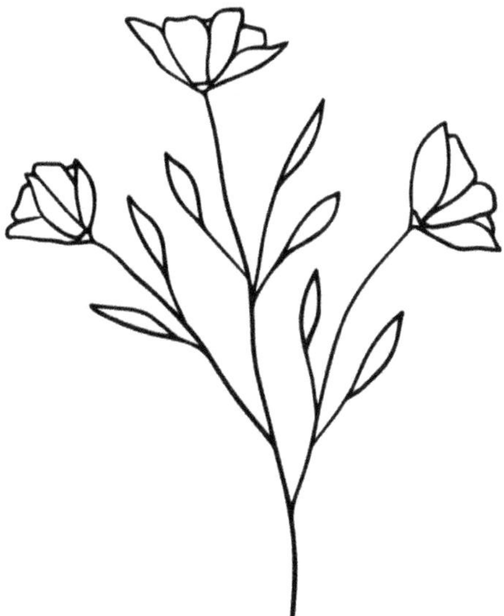

i long to feel your skin - against mine
i can feel you in my thoughts,
i can taste you in my dreams
lately, my favorite place to be

i've never felt so seen,
so known
a simple magic all its own
the cryptic messages...
ingrained in our skin,
you reach for me
and i let you in

nothing goes unspoken,
when the colors begin to show
thought and reason seem to
slip out the door,
i'm ready for something more
i stare at your sleeping face,
wondering what it is you're waiting for

all emotions,
one fluid motion
it sways and swirls
your hands lost in my curls
an endless sea
of entangled morals

an intricate collaboration
    of lips and fingers
    woven together
    you - sinking into my chest
whispering sweet incantations
with every last breath

eye to eye - soul to soul,
all dimensions... beyond our control

it's as if our souls
are linked in other dimensions,
it is our bodies that are unfamiliar

centuries of history flooding back
as i feel your hand gently fall down my back

lost in your gaze
the rhythmic sway,
rolling like waves
slowly crashing over me
a few moments here
and then i cave
swept away with the tides
too late to save

i just want you - in my places
will you fill all the spaces?
leave no cracks
for hiding places
no light to shine through
none to spill out into this dark room
do you promise to cover all the bases?

a deep breath in,
slow to let it out,
let it out right over your mouth
our lips caress,
you breathe me in
i could replay these moments
over and over again
you reach for me,
i let you in
warm to the touch,
skin against skin
whispers of longing,
a deep breath in,
all worth the wait in the end

can we stay here?
in this dimly lit room...
where time stands still
and so slowly we move?
small caresses,
salty taste of skin
light whispers, kisses
inviting you in

a free fall into the abyss...
what ignites so much fear around this?
we search and never find
just wasting time...
out of thin air - here i am
running my hand through your hair...
scared to death, but trying not to care

here it comes,
i can feel the burning in my lungs
gripping my chest,
you know the rest...
a crippling feeling, maybe you can guess?
it always comes when
i’m not doing my best
it’s time for change,
for growth,
for rest.
it's time to leave it all behind,
time for a reset

i miss the way our scents combine
that simple moment,
when we are intertwined
so sickly sweet, i feel the drip
of your sweat on me

drop after drop, it rolls down to the sheets
never to be seen, lost...
in a sea of you and i

an anxious mind,
a beating heart...
where do i even start
but here we are...
i know too much
to remain the same
a winner of a losing game

i'll meet you where the water meets the sky
mountains of clouds shifting above the tides
the taste of salt on my skin
watch as our hair blows in the wind
diving deep into the blue, first the sun meets our eyes
then, i find you

a wave of emotion
rolling out into the ocean
i keep coming up for air
i keep realizing you're not there
open my eyes to see
every shade of blue
none of them come close
to matching the hue
that i love gazing into
a breath - a gasp
let this be my last
i dive into the depths
where my heart is kept
...shipwrecked

diving deep into the treacherous blue,
will i swim, will i float? will i drown?
would i even know?
i crave the consistency of the waves,
crashing over me,
my bare skin
the waves, they always come back
again and again... luring me in
they pull me under so fast, so deep
instant relief, fully surrounded - immersed
i am yours to keep...
everything i've always sought and known
you can find me here, deep in the treacherous blue
the treacherous blue that i call my own.

i play games like
connect the dots,
with all your freckles
while pondering thoughts,
thoughts of you
thoughts of me...
thoughts of us...
together & separately

every time my eyes find yours
i just want to melt into you
open all of the secret doors
and get lost so deep inside of you
feel the warmth of your skin against mine
and be ignited by you
a fire that burns so bright
i can't be denied by you

in a sea of clutched faces & warm skin
i can't get enough,
from beginning... to end
i give it all that i have
and all that i know
we are only here momentarily
to stay warm while it snows
the panic is gone
and the snow starts to slow
the lights come back on,
and i know
the time has come,
i must go

every limb wound together,
every finger interlaced
snow dancing down,
past the silhouette of your face
only light slow movements
no need to stir
time stops, standing still
here in our secret place

crystalized,
lost in a sea of glazed over eyes
you lost me before our last goodbye

life is so peculiar, as it ebbs and flows
constantly in forward motion,
steady as it goes
so much time spent looking forward and back
a subtle notion of the presence we lack
i can see the unrest as it tries to hide
hide behind those ice blue eyes,
that gaze down into mine
i try to slow my pace,
to wait,
but you can't rewind time
this just isn't our fate

all the pieces
have begun to fall
i look around, to see
that there are no more walls

nothing to keep me safe,
safe from myself
or anyone else

crumbling down
with such loud sounds
reverberating, as the pieces
hit the ground

i've been lost for so long,
i don't know if i want to be found.

always say the words that harvest in your mind,
you never know
who will come to find
to find that your words
hold the key
the key to whom
they need to be
we are all just wanderers here
wanderers, waiting for someone
to help us steer
steer our sails into the wind
the wind catches hold
and off we go again
another adventure with words untold
it's time to speak and let the journey unfold

i am the creator of this world
this world i call my own
i am the creator of this place
a place i call my home
i am the maker of my dreams
dreams that will soon become known

i paint in words and think in dreams
dreaming of lovely, flow-y things
spinning around and growing wings
life is soft and sharp and sweet
i see you, and you see me
spinning round and round we see
all of the things
all of the lovely flow-y things
i let go and you dive deep
head first we spiral,
what a heavenly dream.

daughter of the moon,
keeper of the stars
all that is good,
is all that you are
never lose sight of what this shows
your father, the moon
may be far...
but he is always watching you glow.

human connection,
the lost art
everything in the world trying to pull us apart
we must rise, together
there is an end in sight
just remember it is your humane right
to experience this life

sonder creeps,
as the light begins to reach
to reach her restful eyes
they begin to flutter,
the moment, subtle & brief...
she begins to see,
to see that she has never been alone,
not in the way she thinks
every thought...
so subtle, so brief.

what is the essence you hold?
i can't place it,
the air is far too cold
shivering; i reach... for anything
emanating warmth outside of these sheets
limerence begins to fade,
as the facade falls away
just another cold, rainy day

we live in vivid complexity,
alone - with you right next to me
heavy winds of emotion
blurring such a simplistic notion
again, sonder appears
and sets new thoughts
and waves into motion

day in and day out
we walk around
all these noises in our heads,
but we never make a sound
imagine a world where
we spoke our minds
imagine a world full of honesty
with no more wasted time
imagine a world,
where you could be mine

loss is inevitable,
its all i knew, all i know
which is why i have to let you go
forever trying to return home,
to the only feeling i know
a place where i always end up alone,
space to be who i need to be...
all that i knew, all that i know
all that i... am

its that time again,
that time to shed my skin
recreate who i am,
without this great sadness that lies within

its that time again
that time to trust in the stars
recreate all the scars,
the scars who tell us stories
of who we are

this chaos has hindered my soul
from reaching equilibrium
here i stay in a constant
state of delirium
waiting for the clouds to clear,
the sun to shine
stuck here, here in this moment in time

flashes of faces
a million smiles
a highlight reel that goes on for miles
love and laughs,
always running through my mind
all the love that had to be left behind
an accumulation, a culmination
of all of the lovely words and lips
... i could momentarily call mine

i write to bring you back to life,
to feel your heart - beat
next to mine
to remember what it felt like
to be intertwined

if her body were the page
what stories would your lips be writing
would this last for days
or be quick to fade?
over long before it even started?
does it get better with age?
or would it become jaded
with the lonely hearted?

the love that you hold for yourself,
is the sweetest love of all
so tangible, so real
no one gets hurt when you fall
we only rise, as our cup overflows
such a sensual experience as it comes & goes
realizing that you, are all you'll ever need
to grow

life flows at a continuous current,
just as the streams

no looking back or slowing,
always at a constant speed

sometimes the serenity nature
has to offer, is just
what we need.

i learned so much with you,
about life and myself too
i miss those nights with you
i can see it in your eyes,
you miss them too
a touch so familiar,
a thought... so peculiar
it feels like we're eons apart,
even though you couldn't be nearer
i can feel your smile, i don't even need to see your face
how comfortable with you here-in my space
what a distant place

we spend lifetimes hiding
from the pains of the past
deep down we know,
it will never last
a steady pace
we run and run
only to look up to find
how little we've done
we've never left this space
all this pain, it must be faced
or we will forever be running in place

it takes time,
loving yourself...
take your place in line
to learn yourself
it's always worth the find
to uncover yourself
it's always worth the wait;
you are always worth the wait

a deep sigh of relief
years of holding the same breath,
too scared to breathe
today is the day,
she is almost complete
years and years of
rinse and repeat
here we stand - so much closer
to the masterpiece

emotions, more like music
songs from the past
i always like to sit and listen
they never seem to last
we play them on repeat
just to bring them back
just a distant memory
a reminder of the things we can never get back

i sit here and stare into an empty space
mind blank, heart racing
a game of give and take
i've far exceeded the limit
my heart begins to ache
i'm at a loss for words, even thoughts
why are we here?
what is this place?

light me on fire,
the brightest of flames,
let me warm you with desire
a sight i assure you, you've never seen
i'll show you a map of all the places i've ever been
then burn it to your skin so you will never forget the way again.

i see him, but i can only think of you
i miss the touch of your lips against my skin,
i miss the way we laughed,
the warmth of your hands pulling me in
i miss the comfortable silences,
basking in your unspoken words
feeling all of the emotions that you would
never speak to life,
an unwavering notion,
all this tension you could cut with a knife
all the while knowing
you not so secretly loved having me in your life.

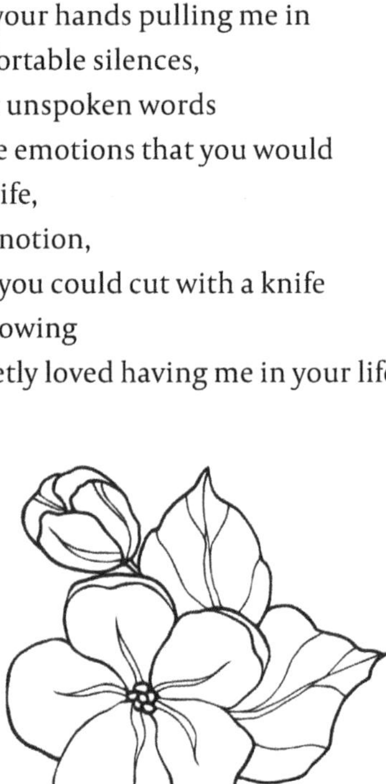

there i stood,
the wind blowing in all directions
water crashing at my feet
the tide rolling to perfection
arms outreached
the sky draws me in
i don't know if i will ever feel this free again
i close my eyes and take the moment in
i can feel the power in my palms
the energy of the stars; cosmic release
the dark sky whispers, "you are free...
free to be all that you are,
your power will never cease
my daughter, you are made from the stars."

life, just a bunch of laser cut wooden pieces
waiting for a pivotal shift
to fall into place
always holding space
a minute part of a much larger picture
how long will it take?
to unlock the doors in your mind
how long will it take?
for the puzzle of life to fall into place

something so real - so genuine
something unreal - so intimate
i feel like a child again
so pure - so innocent
here i stand,
so lost - so impotent

transcending through space and time
pivotal shifts... not yours, but mine
here we stand at the end of the line
no one's fault... not yours, not mine
it’s not always until the end of time
after all... time is an illusion
just as you, and i

the water pours down, over my eyes
my lips find yours by surprise
a simple touch
in this moment, i want you so much
i feel your hands fall down my skin,
i reach for you - you pull me in
i feel your mind
clearing, of all other thought
you're here, fully here
you're usually not
i welcome your embrace
quick to realize this may be the only time we've got
i can see it in your eyes,
a flicker of need - a small glimpse of love
hidden behind the walls,
these walls encasing your heart
i've been climbing for days
i slip and fall , why do you make this so hard
if i reach the top, could i make it through the gates?
these gates of your heart,
next time will you give me a head-start?

an unspoken trust
emanating between
the two of us
both slow to say
what it is that lingers
beneath our eyes
similar pains of the past
keeping us from what may
the chemistry runs deep
my legs spread
as you grab my thighs
i crave your... touch
almost as much
as a crave your... mind

let all the noise fade
be here with me
caught in my gaze
i want to feel your heart
sync with mine
be here with me
for this moment in time

freedom is found
in the slow down
peace in the presence,
let it all go
sit here in silence with me
for the first time in years
a feeling of ease,
a feeling of peace,
pure alignment
i no longer seek,
knowing i'm exactly where
i am meant to be

bare-feet pressed against the cool stone,
looking out to the world unknown
slowly warmed by the suns rays
diamonds on the water,
some would say, it's the perfect day
a brisk wind reminding me of the seasons change
pure bliss -a silent kiss
not a thought on my mind, not a cloud in the sky

i wish to be well,
i wish to be full...
i wish to show and tell,
all of my love for you

have you seen her?
the way that she radiates
she no longer placates...
ready to vacate,
the shell that she inhabits
the petals burst through
as she blooms

About The Author

Sierra Lewis may be a first time author, but you would never know based on her passion for writing and connecting with people. *Wildflowers* is a collection of poems written as a way for her to embody her emotions inspired by real life experiences and all the souls she's met along the way.

CPSIA information can be obtained
at www.ICGtesting.com
Printed in the USA
LVHW020729260323
742606LV00001B/6

9 781637 903964